AGE

by

Grace Jones

BookLife
PUBLISHING

©This edition was
published in 2022.
First published in 2017.

BookLife Publishing Ltd,
King's Lynn, Norfolk
PE30 4LS, UK

ISBN: 978-1-80155-678-1

A catalogue record for this book
is available from the British Library.

Written by:
Grace Jones

Edited by:
Charlie Ogden

Designed by:
Drue Rintoul

All facts, statistics, web addresses and URLs in this book were verified as valid and
accurate at time of writing. No responsibility for any changes to external websites or
references can be accepted by either the author or publisher.

CONTENTS

Words that look like **this** can be found in the glossary on page 31.

THE BRONZE AGE

*THE BRONZE AGE BEGAN AROUND 3000 **BC** AND IT MARKS A PERIOD OF HISTORY WHEN PEOPLE BEGAN TO MAKE OBJECTS OUT OF METAL.*

The first metal that people used to make things out of was copper and most of the Early Bronze Age **artefacts** that have survived to this day are made from it. During the Middle to Late Bronze Age, people discovered that copper could be mixed with another metal, tin, to make bronze. Bronze was much harder than copper and could be used to make stronger tools and weapons.

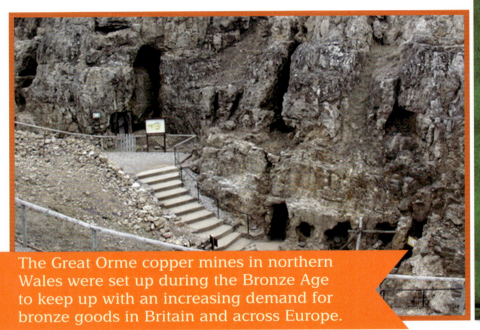

The Great Orme copper mines in northern Wales were set up during the Bronze Age to keep up with an increasing demand for bronze goods in Britain and across Europe.

WHAT DOES PREHISTORIC MEAN?

PREHISTORIC MEANS THAT WE HAVE NO WRITTEN RECORDS FROM THE TIME. PREHISTORIC PEOPLE IN BRITAIN HAD NO WRITTEN LANGUAGE, MEANING THAT THEY COULDN'T WRITE ANYTHING DOWN. BECAUSE OF THIS, **ARCHAEOLOGISTS** AND **HISTORIANS** STUDY THE MANY ARTEFACTS, ARTWORKS, **RUINS** AND SKELETONS FROM THE PERIOD, AS THESE CAN TELL US ABOUT LIFE IN THE BRONZE AGE AND THE IRON AGE.

HOW WERE BRONZE OBJECTS MADE?

Copper and tin, the metals that are used to make bronze, had to be extracted from rock. Rocks that contain metals are known as ores. Prehistoric metalworkers would crush the copper or tin ore until the metal was released. The metals would then have been heated over a fire at an extremely high temperature until they melted, a process called smelting. The liquid metal would have been poured into moulds or shaped individually by hand into bronze tools, weapons, **vessels**, display objects or ornate pieces of jewellery.

A Bronze Age sword, called a rapier, that was found in Cambridgeshire, England

LIFE IN THE BRONZE AGE

Life in the Bronze Age was much more advanced than in the Stone Age. This was mostly because Bronze Age people could use bronze to make better tools for farming and building. As well as this, the Bronze Age saw people trading with each other for the first time. Bronze Age people would travel across Britain and Europe to trade important **commodities**, such as gold and amber, in return for bronze tools, weapons and jewellery.

A Late Bronze Age golden oath ring dated to around 950–700 BC

Most people at the beginning of the Bronze Age only lived with their families, but this changed and people started to live with other families in small village communities. The Bronze Age was also the first time that there had been a social difference between people; as some were rich and some were poor. Most rich communities got their money from trading bronze and copper items within Britain and Europe.

This amber and jet necklace, dated to around 1500 BC, was discovered in Cambridgeshire, England.

THE BEAKER PEOPLE

THE BEAKER PEOPLE LIVED DURING THE BRONZE AGE. They have been named after the highly-distinctive, bell-shaped beakers they made.

They first appeared in western Europe around 2800 BC and were one of the earliest known groups of people to use metal to make tools and other objects. Much of what we know about the Beaker people's culture comes from human remains and artefacts, such as Beaker pots, tools and weapons. These artefacts have been found in the graves of Beaker people at burial sites across Britain and Europe.

This replica Beaker pot shows the distinctive style of pottery that the Beaker people were known to produce.

The Amesbury Archer

The Amesbury Archer was an Early Bronze Age man whose skeleton was **excavated** from a burial site near Stonehenge. He is believed to have lived around 4,300 years ago and originally came from an area near to the **Alps**, perhaps travelling long distances to England to trade goods. He was buried with around 100 objects including Beaker pots, **flint** arrowheads, copper knives and gold hair ornaments. Because of the number and value of the objects he was buried with, historians think he was probably a rich **trader**.

This picture shows the skeleton of the Amesbury Archer and some of the goods that were buried with him, including the distinctive Beaker pots.

THE AMESBURY ARCHER HAS BEEN NICKNAMED THE 'KING OF STONEHENGE', AS HISTORIANS BELIEVE HE WAS A RICH AND POWERFUL MAN DURING THE EARLY BRONZE AGE.

TRADE AND TRAVEL

The remains of a 3,000 year old Bronze Age wooden log boat, which would have been used by the Beaker people to transport their goods by sea

The Beaker people were thought to be the first real explorers and travellers in the prehistoric period. Beaker culture is believed to have been brought to Britain from other parts of western Europe in around 2500 BC. Beaker people are believed to be one of the first groups of people to learn how to smelt metals such as copper, bronze and gold, as well as produce pottery. They would have transported their items across the seas using wooden log boats and then traded them for other goods.

Beaker Pots

Beaker pots are believed to have been very important to Beaker culture. They all have a similar bell-style shape and many of them have the same grooved and dotted patterns on them. They would have been made out of clay before being placed in a fire in order to harden them into pottery. They would have been used to hold food, mead, beer and other drinks.

Bell-shaped, patterned Beaker pot

INVENTIONS AND TECHNOLOGY

THE BRONZE AGE WAS A TIME OF SIGNIFICANT TECHNOLOGICAL ADVANCEMENT AND GREAT INNOVATION.

TRANSPORT AND TRAVEL

In 2016, the oldest wheel ever found in Britain was uncovered at a Bronze Age archaeological site in East Anglia. The wheel dates back to around 1100–800 BC and is one metre in diameter. The wheel had been well preserved by the **silt** in the ground at the archaeological site.

Archaeologists believe that the wheel was once part of the earliest known vehicle, the horse-drawn cart, as horse bones were also found at the site. Horse-drawn carts would have meant that food, weapons and building materials could have been transported more quickly.

The Uffington White Horse can be found on a hillside in Oxfordshire and dates back to the prehistoric period. It is made from deep trenches filled to the top with crushed white chalk. Historians are not quite sure why it is there, or even whether it actually is a horse, but some believe it represents the importance of horses and transport within Bronze Age society.

Over 15 Bronze Age boats have been discovered in Britain, many of which are log boats. These boats would have been built from oak planks that were sewn together with tough yew branches and fixed with wooden wedges.

New advances in boat-making would have allowed Beaker people to travel to Britain and begin to settle. It would have also opened up new routes to trade bronze and copper goods in Europe.

Tools and Weapons

In the Early Bronze Age, the discovery of metal meant that people could create much stronger and longer-lasting tools and weapons. Miners collected different types of metal, mostly copper and tin, and metalworkers used them to make and craft objects. Some objects could be used for a lot of different things and often everyday tools became useful weapons in battle.

Axes would have been used to chop down trees and cut logs into smaller pieces, which could then have been used as a building material or firewood. However, they would have also been used as fearsome weapons in times of war. Metalworkers hammered the edges of axe heads and created thin sockets in the handle in order to securely attach the axe head to the **shaft**.

This Bronze Age axe head was found in Wisbech, England, and the marks made by the hammer that was used to shape it can still be seen.

This typical example of a Bronze Age dagger was found in Cambridgeshire, England.

Bronze daggers were particularly popular during the Bronze Age and were used as a light-weight weapon that could cut through small objects or stab people during wartime. They were also important as a means of showing off a person's wealth and status and would often have been polished in order to give the effect of a golden surface.

THERE HAVE BEEN MANY OTHER WEAPONS FOUND BURIED IN THE GRAVES OF BRONZE AGE WARRIORS, INCLUDING SPEARS, ARROWHEADS, SHIELDS, BOWS AND SWORDS.

EVERYDAY LIFE

EVERYDAY LIFE IN THE BRONZE AGE WAS A LOT BETTER THAN LIFE IN THE STONE AGE. People who lived during the Bronze Age had more food, better houses to live in and a greater range of food and weapons.

Village People

Bronze Age families usually lived with other families in small village communities. These communities were often made up of several families and usually had a village leader. Most people would have spent their time farming, raising livestock and growing and harvesting crops, such as wheat and barley.

However, villages may have also had a number of skilled tradespeople who could have been metalworkers, miners, weavers or potters. Villagers' social lives would have been centred around the home, with families and communities cooking and eating together, sharing stories and perhaps even playing games.

HOMES

Families in the late Bronze Age would have lived in round huts with cone-shaped roofs. Buildings like this are known as roundhouses. The walls would have been built using wood that had been plastered with mud. The roofs would have been **thatched**, meaning that they would have been made out of tightly-packed bundles of straw or grass. Together, the combination of the mud plaster and the thatched roof would have made these houses waterproof and warm. There would have been one room inside each house with a **hearth** in the middle that could have been used for cooking, warmth and light.

This reconstruction of what a typical Bronze Age roundhouse would have looked like was built at Flag Fen, East Anglia, England.

FLAG FEN

In 2006, archaeologists began to excavate a site in East Anglia, England. Since then, they have uncovered one of the largest and best-preserved Bronze Age settlements ever found in Britain. It has been named Flag Fen and the land is believed to have been first settled on around 3,500 years ago.

The discoveries made at Flag Fen have helped to confirm much of what we now know about Bronze Age settlements and everyday life. So far, archaeologists have uncovered glass beaded pots, parts of roundhouses, weapons, tools and the stored remains of grain, bones and even human faeces (poo). All of this reveals important information about what everyday life was like for the settlers of Flag Fen.

Rising sea levels meant that the land around Flag Fen became flooded by the Middle Bronze Age. In 1300 BC, raised paths, called causeways, were built from planks of wood so that the people could still walk around Flag Fen. The causeways at Flag Fen were made out of around 60,000 wooden planks. The dead were also buried in the marshes by the causeways with grave goods such as weapons, tools and pottery.

SO MANY ARTEFACTS HAVE BEEN FOUND AT FLAG FEN BECAUSE THE CLAY QUARRY THAT THEY WERE BURIED IN HAS KEPT THEM VERY WELL-PRESERVED.

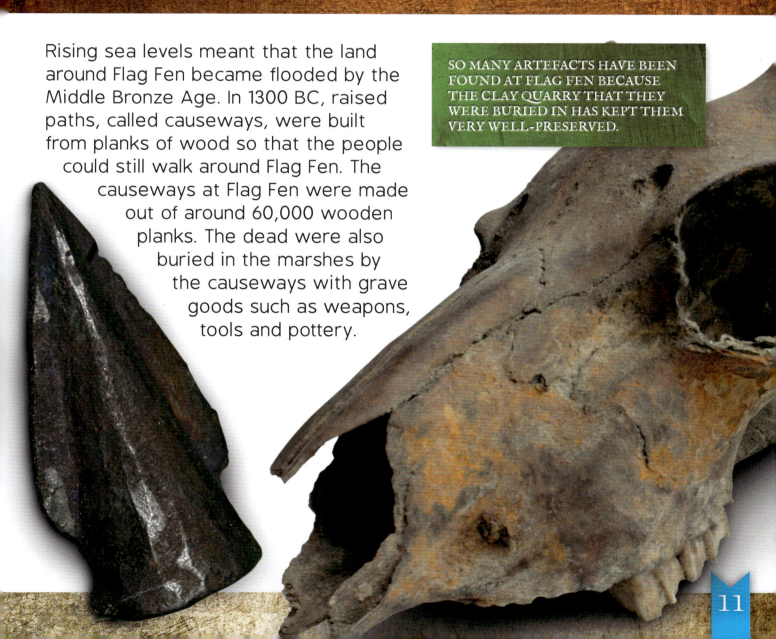

STONEHENGE

STONE HENGES CONTINUED TO BE BUILT THROUGHOUT THE BRONZE AGE. The most famous prehistoric henge in Britain is called Stonehenge and it is located in Wiltshire, England.

Stonehenge is around 5,000 years old, its construction starting in the Early Bronze Age. It was built in several stages over hundreds of years. Historians are still not sure exactly why Stonehenge was built, but many believe Stonehenge may have been used for religious ceremonies, as a burial ground and for **rituals** that mark the changing of the seasons.

Stonehenge

Stonehenge Wasn't Built in a Day ...

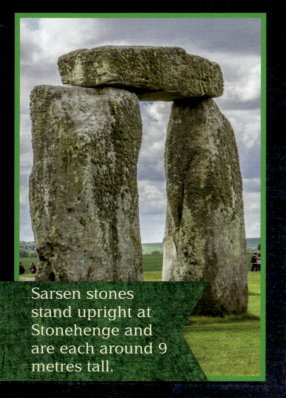

Sarsen stones stand upright at Stonehenge and are each around 9 metres tall.

Two types of stone were used to construct Stonehenge — bluestones, which are the smaller stones, and sarsens, which are larger and made out of sandstone. Stonehenge consists of two circles that were built at different times; an inner circle built from sarsens and an outer circle built from bluestones. Around 2150 BC, 82 bluestones were transported hundreds of kilometres from the Preseli mountains in south-west Wales to build the outer circle. In around 2000 BC, the sarsen stones were added to the monument and were transported from the closer Marlborough Downs in north Wiltshire, England, over 32 kilometres away. To this day, it still remains a mystery how the prehistoric people were able to move the huge stones over such long distances.

Dead and Buried

Many archaeologists and historians believe that Stonehenge may have functioned as a burial ground. This is because around 65 **cremated** human remains have been found at the site and as many as 150 people are believed to have been originally buried there, making it the largest prehistoric cemetery in Britain. Some people believe the stones commemorate the deaths of important members of the same family, community or religious order because of the size of the monument and the effort taken to build it.

SUMMER AND WINTER SOLSTICES

Some people also believe that religious ceremonies took place every year at Stonehenge to mark the summer solstice in June and the winter solstice in December. Solstices occur twice every year when the Sun reaches its highest or lowest point in the sky. These are also the longest and shortest days of the year. Some historians believe that the position of the stones links to the position of the Sun during both the summer and winter solstices. Solstice festivals still take place at Stonehenge for this reason.

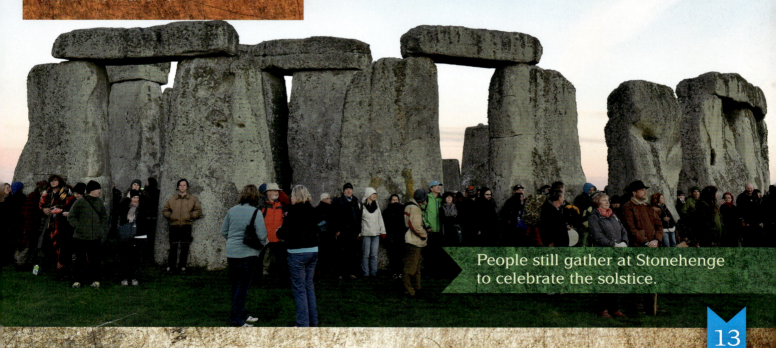

People still gather at Stonehenge to celebrate the solstice.

THE IRON AGE

AFTER THE BRONZE AGE CAME THE IRON AGE, WHICH BEGAN IN BRITAIN AROUND 800 BC. It marks a period of history when people began to make objects out of iron.

Although this period of history is known for its ironwork, iron technology only became widespread in Britain around 600 BC. People in other parts of the world knew how to work iron many years before this. Throughout the Iron Age, metalworkers continued to make objects out of other metals, including bronze, gold and silver. Iron was used to make lots of different things, especially tools and weapons, as it is harder and more **durable** than bronze. Gold and silver would have mostly been used to make jewellery and coins.

This gold **torc** found in Needwood Forest, England, dates back to around 75 BC.

How Were Iron Objects Made?

As in the Bronze Age with copper and tin, iron had to be mined and then extracted from iron ores. As with making bronze, the iron ores would have had to have been heated to a very high temperature. However, as iron has a much higher melting temperature than bronze, iron objects were made by a process called forging. This meant that **blacksmiths** had to cut, bend, twist and hammer the iron into the correct shape using an **anvil** and a hammer. Blacksmiths were very important in Iron Age society and the most skilled blacksmiths could become powerful people within their community.

This iron sword dates back to around 60 BC.

Life in the Iron Age

Over the course of the Iron Age, technology and inventions became much more advanced. The introduction of iron allowed for more durable tools and weapons to be crafted. Access to new building materials, improvements in farming techniques and the introduction of new crops meant that everyday life significantly improved for people during the Iron Age.

At this time, Britain (and much of Europe) was made up of small communities called **tribes**. While the tribes were different from each other in many ways, they all shared a similar culture and way of life. The tribes that spread across Britain and much of Europe are known today as the Celts.

This is a replica of what a Celtic warrior might have worn during the Iron Age.

THE POPULATION OF BRITAIN DURING THE IRON AGE IS ESTIMATED TO HAVE INCREASED TO OVER ONE MILLION PEOPLE. THIS IS BECAUSE IMPROVEMENTS IN FARMING AND TECHNOLOGY MADE LIFE A LOT EASIER.

A reconstruction of an Iron Age home, called a roundhouse, at the Iron Age site of Bodrifty Farm, England.

THE CELTS

THE CELTS WERE MADE UP OF DIFFERENT TRIBES THAT LIVED ACROSS EUROPE DURING THE IRON AGE. While the Celtic way of life is thought to have begun as early as 1200 BC in parts of Europe, it only reached Britain around 600 BC.

WHO WERE THE CELTS?

2,500 years ago, the Celts occupied large parts of Europe. Each Celtic tribe had their own individual identity, traditions, beliefs and practices, but they also shared a common culture and way of life.

For example, the tribes spoke many different languages, but all of the languages were similar and related to one another. Today, they are called the Celtic languages.

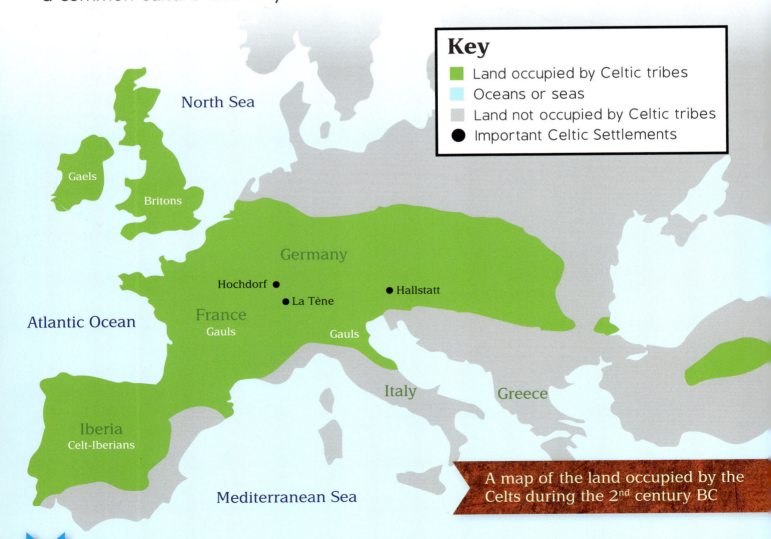

Key
- Land occupied by Celtic tribes
- Oceans or seas
- Land not occupied by Celtic tribes
- ● Important Celtic Settlements

North Sea

Gaels

Britons

Germany

Hochdorf ●

● La Tène

● Hallstatt

Atlantic Ocean

France
Gauls

Gauls

Italy

Greece

Iberia
Celt-Iberians

Mediterranean Sea

A map of the land occupied by the Celts during the 2nd century BC

THE CELTS IN BRITAIN

It is thought that Celtic culture first arrived in Britain around 600 BC and quickly spread throughout the rest of the island. It was introduced by Celtic traders from other parts of Europe. It is thought that the Gauls, the Celtic tribe that lived in France, were probably the first Celts to come to Britain.

The Britons and Gaels

There were two main groups of Celts in Britain during the Iron Age. The Celts that lived in modern-day England and Wales were called Britons and spoke a number of closely related languages that today are called the Brythonic languages. The Celts that lived in Ireland were known as the Gaels and they spoke a number of different languages that today are called the Goidelic languages. On both islands lived a large number of tribes who controlled certain areas of land. These tribes often fought with one another and would raid each other's villages to steal things such as livestock, tools and clothing.

Key

01 Caledones	15 Corieltauvi
02 Taexali	16 Iceni
03 Carvetii	17 Demetae
04 Venicones	18 Catuvellauni
05 Epidii	19 Silures
06 Damnonii	20 Dobunni
07 Novantae	21 Dumnonii
08 Selgovae	22 Durotriges
09 Votadini	23 Belgae
10 Brigantes	24 Atrebates
11 Parisi	25 Regni
12 Cornovii	26 Cantiaci
13 Deceangli	27 Trinovantes
14 Ordovices	

CELTIC SOCIETY

CELTIC TRIBES WERE EACH RULED BY ONE POWERFUL LEADER. The rest of the tribe was divided into an ordered **hierarchy**.

KINGS, QUEENS AND CHIEFTAINS

Tribal rulers in Celtic society, who were known as either kings, queens or chieftains, came from the highest social class and were extremely powerful and wealthy. As war was so important in Celtic society, rulers were usually great warriors and would have led the rest of their tribe into battle during times of war. Most would have **inherited** their titles from their fathers, but some would have been chosen as the best ruler by other high-ranking tribespeople. Unlike most societies at that time, there were many high-ranking women in Celtic societies. Boudica was the queen of a Celtic tribe who ruled over East Anglia and she led her tribe into battle against the Romans in the early first century (for more information see page 27).

Later in the Iron Age, tribes began to produce staters, which were a type of coin. These staters often had images of warriors, horses and leader's heads on them. The gold coins above were made by the Iceni tribe in around 15 BC.

Warriors, Druids and Bards

Warriors, druids and bards were all considered to be in the upper class of Celtic society. War was a large part of the Celtic way of life and culture, meaning that warriors were considered to be very important. They protected the tribe, gained new lands, had the qualities of strength and bravery and were considered to be heroes in Celtic society.

Druids were religious leaders and were responsible for religious ceremonies. They upheld the law and they were considered to be priests, teachers and healers. Bards were poets who wrote down and recited poetry and performed songs on special occasions. Bards often used their talents to pass on stories of the tribe's history.

This is an Iron Age bronze shield known as the Battersea Shield. It was found in England and is believed to have been used during religious ceremonies.

Farmers and Metalworkers

The majority of Celts were farmers and metalworkers. Farmers were very important in Celtic tribes as they provided food and materials for everyone in the tribe. Metalworkers worked to create everyday objects for the tribe, such as tools and weapons, and they produced goods to trade with other tribes in Britain and Europe.

LABOURERS AND SLAVES

The lower classes were mostly made up of labourers who worked on the land to produce crops or raise livestock. These labourers had very few rights and would not have been seen as important. Slaves, however, who had been captured and stolen from other tribes during raids, had no freedom at all.

THE CELTIC SOCIAL HIERARCHY

Kings, Queens and Chieftains

Warriors, Druids and Bards

Farmers and Metalworkers

Labourers and Slaves

HOUSES AND HILL FORTS

MOST CELTS LIVED IN FARMING COMMUNITIES IN SMALL, SCATTERED VILLAGES. These villages were usually surrounded by a bank and a ditch to help to defend them from attacking enemy tribes.

ROUNDHOUSES

Each family usually lived, cooked and socialised together in a roundhouse. Sometimes, families lived in a collection of roundhouses that were built close together. These roundhouses were built using natural and locally available materials. The walls were usually made from wood. Occasionally, stones were put together with a mixture of straw and mud, known as daub, and this was used to make walls as it kept the roundhouses insulated and warm. The roundhouses' cone-shaped roofs were thatched and often had mud placed on top to keep the houses warm.

This reconstruction at the archaeological site of Flag Fen in Cambridgeshire, England, shows what a typical Iron Age roundhouse would have looked like.

What Was Inside a Roundhouse?

Roundhouses had no windows and inside there would have been one big, circular room. In the middle would have been a hearth where a fire, which was constantly tended to, would have been lit to produce light, heat and the means to cook. There was a small hole in the roof where the smoke from the fire could escape. As well as this, there would have probably been a loom to weave cloth, a quern stone for grinding corn and an oven to bake bread. Families would have slept in beds that consisted of hay mattresses and woollen blankets. The animals would have often been brought inside the house at night to keep them warm and safe from thieves and raiders.

This is a reconstruction of what the inside of a roundhouse might have looked like.

Hill Forts

Hill forts were human-made settlements built on the top of large hills. They were surrounded by deep ditches and defensive walls. Their towering position made it easy for Celts inside a hill fort to quickly see invading enemies and defend against them. It is estimated that the Celts built over 3,200 hill forts in Britain.

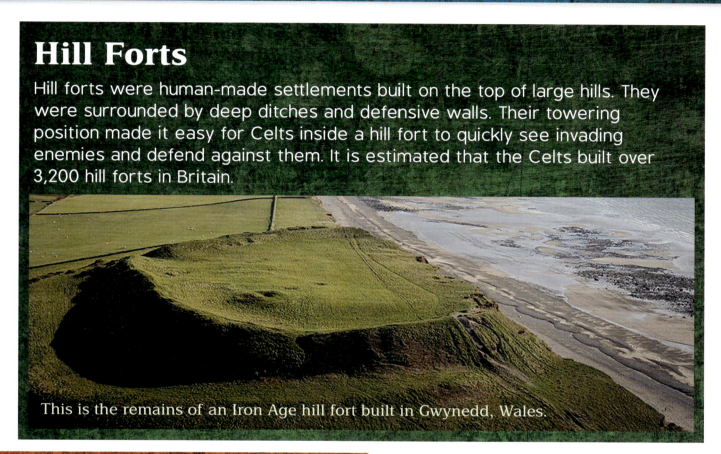

This is the remains of an Iron Age hill fort built in Gwynedd, Wales.

An aerial view of Maiden Castle, England

MAIDEN CASTLE GETS ITS NAME FROM THE CELTIC WORD 'MAI DUN', WHICH MEANS 'GREAT HILL'.

MAIDEN CASTLE

Maiden Castle, the largest Iron Age hill fort in Europe, is located in Dorset, England. It was first built around 600 BC, but in 450 BC major building work was undertaken to extend the area and make the **ramparts** and ditches bigger. The hill fort was occupied until at least the 1st century **AD** and was, at that point, home to a Celtic tribe called the Durotriges.

WAR AND WARRIORS

MUCH OF CELTIC LIFE AND CULTURE REVOLVED AROUND WARFARE. Celtic warriors were considered by most to be brave and fearless heroes.

CELTIC WARRIORS

Nearly all Celts were warriors. During battles, every person in the tribe needed to rally together in order to defeat the enemy. While women usually stayed at home to look after the crops and children, they could choose to train and fight as warriors if they wanted to. Most Celtic men trained to be warriors from a very young age and they were extremely skilled at fighting.

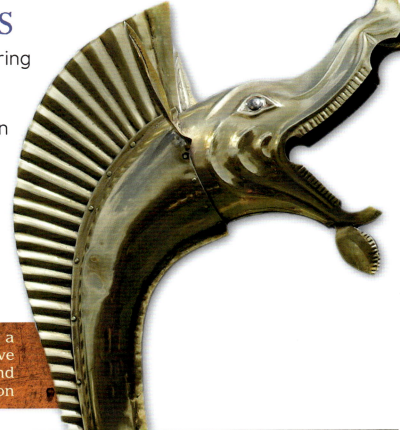

A replica of a war trumpet, called a carnyx, that Celtic warriors would have blown before a battle began or to sound victory when a battle had been won

What Did They Wear?

Often warriors would fight entirely naked and without protection, but many also wore a few basic items to help to protect themselves in battle. They wore bronze helmets, which occasionally had horns on them. Some covered themselves in armour made from iron chains, called a mail shirt, that would have been made by their tribe's blacksmiths. They would have carried oval-shaped shields made of wood or bronze that would have had a central strip of iron in them to make them stronger.

WHAT WEAPONS DID THEY USE?

When Iron Age men and women went to battle, they would have been most likely to fight using swords. These swords would have been made from iron. While most Celts would have owned a simple sword, richer and more important Celts would have owned beautifully decorated swords. More skilled Celtic warriors would have fought using iron spears. Spears would have been difficult and time-consuming to make, so only those who were very talented at using them would have fought with them.

Iron Age spear tips

Fearsome Warriors

Celtic warriors are considered to be some of the most fearsome and fearless warriors of all time. This is partly because they used tactics to terrify their enemies. Before a battle began, one warrior would blow the carnyx while the others beat their swords against their shields and screamed battled cries at the enemy. They would also ride into battle on horses wearing large bronze or wooden horned helmets, screaming all the while. There are even accounts that suggest that Celtic warriors bleached their hair and spiked it into horns.

Often fighting naked or bare-chested, some Celts decorated their bare skin with tattoos using a blue dye made from the woad plant. If they were successful in battle, Celts would chop off the head of the enemy tribe's chieftain and hang it from their belts or in their temples. Many Celts believed that the heads of great leaders and warriors had magical qualities. All of this added to the Celts' reputation as fearsome warriors.

RELIGION AND BURIAL

MOST ARCHAEOLOGISTS BELIEVE THAT THE CELTS WERE POLYTHEISTIC. This means that they believed in many different gods, each of which had different powers and abilities. The leaders of Celtic religions were called druids and they would perform religious ceremonies and sacrifice animals to the gods.

SACRIFICES

One of the main ways that Celts worshipped their gods was through sacrifices. Usually, this simply meant giving valuable objects to the gods, often such things as food, weapons and animal skins. It is believed that these items were often given to the gods by being thrown into lakes and rivers, as the Celts viewed such places as being very special.

This is Llyn Cerrig Bach, a lake on the island of Anglesey in Wales. Over 150 Iron Age artefacts have been found in this lake, including spearheads, swords and helmets. This would seem to show that Iron Age Celts used the lake as a place to sacrifice weaponry to the gods.

On other occasions, the Celts performed live sacrifices. Live sacrifices would have involved killing animals and giving their bodies to the gods as an offering. For many years, historians believed that humans were sacrificed during the Iron Age. However, many historians now believe that the Romans made this up. It's argued that the Romans might have done this to make the Celts seem more savage, which would have made the people back in Rome care less about killing them.

This Iron Age horned helmet was found in the River Thames, suggesting that it may have been an offering to a god. It is the only Iron Age horned helmet ever to be found in Europe.

The Celts often used burial mounds to bury their dead. They also used burial urns, which are jars that hold the remains of a dead person. They would also bury important items alongside the dead and sometimes they would cut off and worship the heads of their ancestors.

This is a reconstructed burial mound of a Celtic chieftain. This is precisely what the burial mound would have looked like when the chieftain was first buried there around 2,500 years ago.

People in the Late Iron Age had a very strong belief in the **afterlife**, so much so that they were often buried with items that were intended to help them in the next life. Items that are buried in graves are known as grave goods. The grave goods in men's graves usually consisted of swords, shields and coins, as these things would help to protect the men in their next life. Women were more likely to be buried alongside jewellery or items used in cooking.

Iron Age people are also known to have worshipped the removed heads of their enemies. Ancient Roman and Greek sources explain that Iron Age people often wore their enemies' heads around their necks.

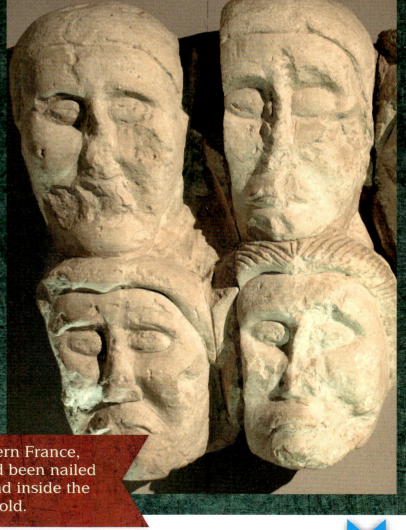

This Celtic pillar fragment, found in southern France, was found to contain actual skulls that had been nailed into place. In total, fifteen skulls were found inside the stone structure, which is over 2,000 years old.

ROMAN INVASION OF BRITAIN

IN AD 40, IRON AGE BRITAIN WAS THE SAME AS IT HAD BEEN FOR HUNDREDS OF YEARS. BUT BY AD 44, LIFE IN BRITAIN HAD BEGUN TO CHANGE.

In AD 43, the Roman Emperor Claudius ordered 20,000 soldiers to land on the south-east coast of England. From there, they moved north and west, fighting the British Celts along the way.

Over the next 40 years, the Romans continued to move throughout Britain, taking control of Celtic tribes and storming numerous hill forts. However, while a lot of people died in the Roman invasion, it also brought about a lot of good.

The first major victory for the Romans was when they succeeded in capturing Camulodunum. Today, we know Camulodunum as Colchester.

This wall in Colchester was built by the Romans and it is still standing today.

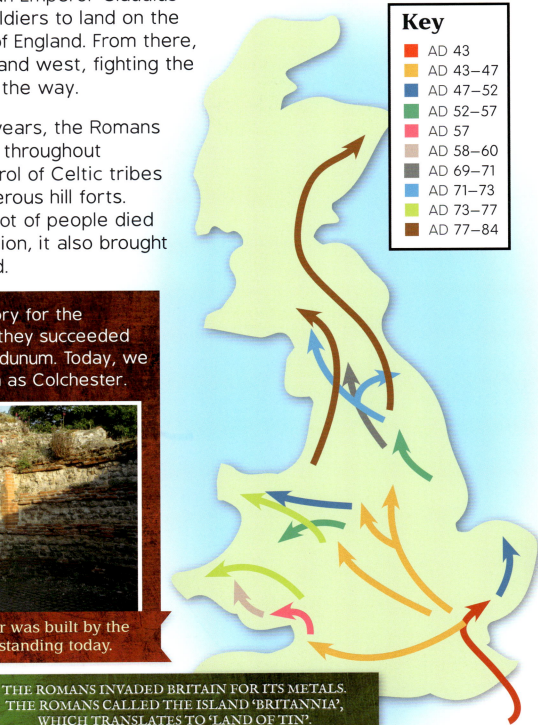

Key
- ■ AD 43
- ■ AD 43–47
- ■ AD 47–52
- ■ AD 52–57
- ■ AD 57
- ■ AD 58–60
- ■ AD 69–71
- ■ AD 71–73
- ■ AD 73–77
- ■ AD 77–84

THE ROMANS INVADED BRITAIN FOR ITS METALS. THE ROMANS CALLED THE ISLAND 'BRITANNIA', WHICH TRANSLATES TO 'LAND OF TIN'.

This ancient Roman road in Portugal is still used by locals today.

THANK YOU ROMANS

The British Celts were actually very lucky that the Romans invaded. This is because the Romans brought with them new food, technology and inventions. These included things such as cabbages, peas and grapes; central heating, plumbing and roads; and cement, libraries and baths.

Boudica

The final battle against the Roman invasion took place in AD 61. After their leader Prasutagus died, the Iceni tribe in East Anglia was treated very badly by the Romans. The Romans took money, land and farm animals from the tribe. Eventually, in AD 61, Prasutagus' wife Boudica decided to fight back against the Romans.

Boudica and her army of 100,000 Celtic rebels attacked both Camulodunum and Londinium. They killed hundreds of Roman soldiers, burnt down temples, destroyed many buildings and left both settlements in ruins.

This statue in London, England, was made to commemorate Boudica and her rebellion against the Romans.

Paintings and drawings of Boudica show her as a mother, a leader and a warrior.

Boudica's final battle against the Romans is known as the Battle of Watling Street. Despite having up to ten times more men than the Romans, the Iceni lost the battle. The Roman army was well-trained and well-rested, whereas Boudica's army had been marching and fighting for many weeks. After defeating Boudica, the Romans ruled southern Britain without any resistance until they left in AD 410.

PREHISTORIC BRITAIN:
A TIMELINE

837,000 BC

The first sign of human life appeared in Britain in Happisburgh, Norfolk.

2500 BC

The building of Stonehenge first began.

2300 BC

The Amesbury Archer is thought to have lived.

2000 BC

Sarsen stones were transported to Stonehenge to complete the final stages of construction.

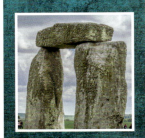

1200 BC

Signs of Celtic-style societies appear in parts of Europe.

STONE AGE

EARLY BRONZE AGE

MIDDLE BRONZE AGE

LATE BRONZE AGE

12,000 BC

The first people began to settle in Britain.

2500 BC

Beaker people began to travel to and settle in Britain.

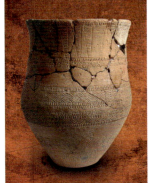

2150 BC

82 bluestones were transported from Wales to Stonehenge.

1500 BC

People began to settle in the large Bronze Age settlement of Flag Fen, England.

1100–800 BC

The oldest wheel ever found in Britain is dated to this period of time.

(It would have looked similar to this one).

1000 BC

The oldest seafaring wooden log boat sailed the seas, before later being found in Dover, England.

800 BC

The Iron Age begins in Britain.

600 BC

Maiden Castle is built in Dorset, England.

150 BC

The Waterloo Helmet, the only Iron Age horned helmet ever found in Britain, was made.

AD 61

Boudica rebels against Roman rule in Britain.

LATE BRONZE AGE

EARLY IRON AGE

LATE IRON AGE

1000–800 BC

The Uffington White Horse in Oxfordshire, England, was built using white chalk.

700 BC

Iron is now used widely across Europe

200 BC

Ironworking in Celtic Europe booms. Iron tools and weapons are made on a larger scale and with greater accuracy.

100 BC

As tribes start to grow and work together, hill forts across Britain fall out of use.

AD 43

The Roman invasion of Britain marks the end of the prehistoric period in Britain with the introduction of the written word.

FIND OUT MORE

WEBSITES

Find out more information about the prehistoric world and the people who lived in it here: **www.bbc.co.uk/history/ancient/british_prehistory**

Unlock the mysteries of Stonehenge by exploring these websites:
www.english-heritage.org.uk/visit/places/stonehenge
www.stonehenge.co.uk/stonehenge

Find out more information about what everyday life was like for the people who lived in an Iron Age village:
www.bbc.co.uk/history/ancient/british_prehistory/ironage_intro_01.shtml

Places to Visit

If you want to learn more about the places and objects that you've just seen, then use these websites to find out how you can visit them for yourself!

Ashmolean Museum
www.ashmolean.org/plan/

British Museum
www.britishmuseum.org/visiting/planning_your_visit.aspx

Flag Fen
https://www.visitpeterborough.com/things-to-do/flag-fen-archaeological-park-p875681

Stonehenge
www.english-heritage.org.uk/visit/places/stonehenge/plan-your-visit/

GLOSSARY

AD	after the birth of Jesus, which is used as the starting point for many calendars around the world
afterlife	a religious belief that there is life after death
Alps	a large mountain range that lies across Europe
anvil	a heavy iron block with a flat top and curved side, on which metal can be hammered and shaped
archaeologists	historians who study buried ruins and ancient objects in order to learn about human history
artefacts	objects made by humans, typically ones of cultural or historical interest
BC	meaning 'before Christ', it is used to mark dates that occurred before the starting year of most calendars
blacksmiths	people who make objects out of iron
commodities	materials or products that can be bought and sold, such as bronze
cremated	to have burnt a dead body to ashes
durable	hard-wearing
excavated	uncovered by digging away and removing the earth that covers it
flint	a hard rock used to make tools during the Stone Age
hearth	the floor of a fireplace
hierarchy	a system where people are ranked in order of power, status or authority
historians	people who study history
inherited	received from a parent after they die
ramparts	defensive walls
rituals	a series of ordered actions that take place during religious ceremonies
ruins	the remains of structures or buildings
shaft	the long, narrow handle of a weapon or tool
silt	fine sand or clay
thatched	a roof cover made out of straw
torc	a neck ornament made of a band of twisted metal, usually gold
trader	a person who trades
tribes	groups of people linked together by family, society, religion or community
vessels	containers used for food or drink

INDEX